Chocolate
at Leisure

by Derrick Tu Tan Pho

AuthorHouse™
1663 Liberty Drive
Bloomington, IN 47403
www.authorhouse.com
Phone: 1-800-839-8640

First published by AuthorHouse 2/22/2011

ISBN: 978-1-4567-4118-1 (sc)

Library of Congress Control Number: 2011902152

Printed in the United States of America

This book is printed on acid-free paper.

author HOUSE®

Table of Contents

Truffles

Chocolate Drinks & Fondue

Cookies

Pâtisserie et Dessert

Basic Recipes

Thank You/Merci

I would like to offer my regards and blessings to all of those who supported me in any respect all these years with a special reference to Cacao Barry/Barry Callebaut Canada.

From Cocoa Bean to Chocolate

I would like to introduce to you the well-known heritage of chocolate making.

The cocoa tree grows to a height of ten to twenty-six feet. The diameter of the trunk is eight to ten inches, and the leaves are oblong and are around eight to twelve inches. The cocoa tree bears buds, flowers, and fruits at the same time. The pods are harvested over a period of several months. In West Africa there are two crops; the main crop extends from October to January and the mid crop from May to July. The cocoa tree grows between twenty degrees north and twenty degrees south latitude. It requires a hot and humid climate and low altitude (2,300 feet maximum). An amazing fact about the flower of the cocoa tree is that it can produce thousands of flowers per season. However, only about forty flowers per tree will eventually develop into cocoa pods. As studies show, the flowers are very selective with regard to pollen, even though they are of the same species; this results in a very low rate of productivity for a fruit tree. This is one of the cost factors of chocolate.

Here are the three varieties of the famous cocoa tree:

- *FORASTERO* is originally from the Amazon and accounts for more than 70 percent of world cocoa production. Forastero is found mainly in western Africa and Brazil. It is a good quality bean, though the chocolate produced from forastero beans has less fine flavor than chocolate produced from criollo and trinitario beans.

- *CRIOLLO* is originally from Central America and some areas of Asia. It accounts for about 5 to 8 percent of world cocoa production. The criollo bean provides a fine chocolate flavor often described as mild, nutty, and full.

TRINITARIO is a hybrid of criollo and forastero that was created in Trinidad and Grenada. It accounts for around twenty percent of world chocolate production. It can be found in some parts of Venezuela and Colombia, Papua New Guinea, and Madagascar. This bean provides a fine chocolate flavor often described as mild, nutty, full, and fruity.

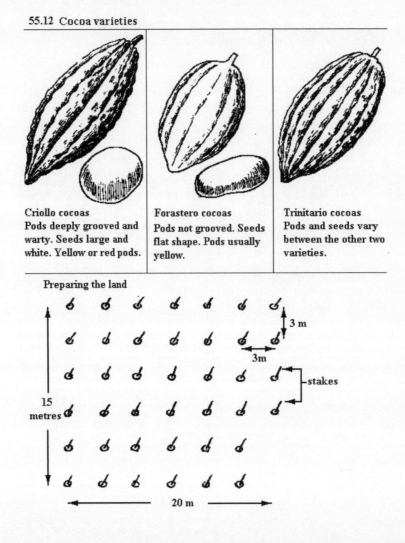

55.12 Cocoa varieties

Criollo cocoas
Pods deeply grooved and warty. Seeds large and white. Yellow or red pods.

Forastero cocoas
Pods not grooved. Seeds flat shape. Pods usually yellow.

Trinitario cocoas
Pods and seeds vary between the other two varieties.

Preparing the land

3 m

3m

stakes

15 metres

20 m

Harvesting:

Cocoa pods are grown on the trunk and main branches of the tree *Theobroma cacao*.

To remove the pods, cocoa farmers use a machete or sharp knife and cut close to the stem. They cannot use their bare hands to pull out the fruit, as it may result in damage to the tree.

De-podding:

De-podding consists of breaking the pods with a piece of wood or a machete and removing the beans and the adhering pulp. De-podding needs to be completed no longer than twenty-four hours after harvesting in order to prevent fermentation of the bean in the pod. After de-podding, the beans and pulp are ready for fermentation.

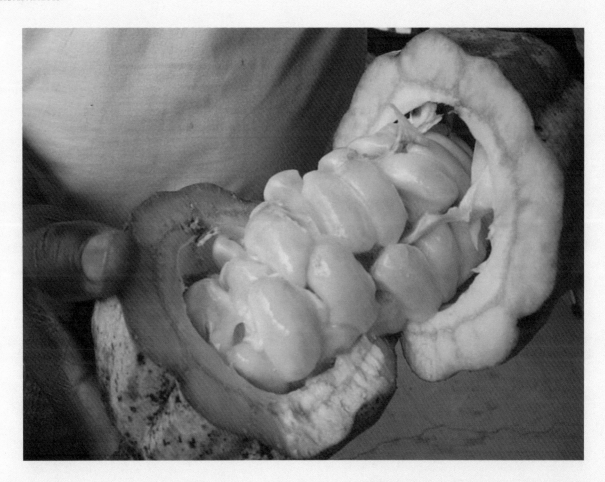

Fermentation and Drying

Fermentation and drying of cocoa is of vital importance. This must start no later than twenty-four hours after de-podding. The objectives of fermentation and drying are to prevent germination of the bean, to separate the grain from the pulp, to initiate chemical and enzymatic reactions inside the beans, to develop flavor and color, and to lower astringency and bitterness.

Fermentation lasts two to seven days; it creates the desired flavor profile while preserving the flavanol in the chocolate.

After fermentation, the beans are placed in trays or on the ground to dry. Sun drying is usually adequate. Banana leaves are used for covering during rainstorms or at night. The drying process reduces the water content from 60 percent to 7 percent.

After a quick cleaning, the cocoa beans are put into bags and prepared for export. The amount exported is listed on the stock market.

When the beans arrive at a chocolate facility, they need to go through the quarantine process for quality assurance, and they go through a cleaning process as well. They are sifted, de-dusted, and de-stoned, and any metal among them is removed. The beans are then winnowed to remove the shells.

Roasting and grinding are critical step that determine the aroma and flavor of the beans. After roasting, the nibs are free of bacteria. They are first ground into a liquor (chocolate at it first stage) and then moved along to the refining process. During refinement, sugar, vanilla lecithin, and milk powder are added if the nibs will be used to make milk chocolate. The process of refining reduces the nibs to a very small particle size for smoothness and silkiness.

The final step is the conching. Conching is a two-phase chocolate-manufacturing process in which the refined chocolate powder is converted to a liquid state through chemical and physical actions. Powder is conched at a specific temperature for a specific time to allow moisture and organic acids to evaporate. During this stage, the chocolate is also flavored and liquefied by adding emulsifier and cocoa butter.

Because cocoa butter is polymorphic, a tempering (or pre-crystallisation) step is needed in order to generate the proper crystal structure. Tempering ensures the following qualities will be present in the final product:

+ Glossy appearance
+ Low incidence of blooming
+ Good "snap"
+ Melting resistance
+ Shelf stability

After tempering, a molding and controlled cooling stage is employed to continue the crystallisation of the cocoa butter into the correct crystal structure.

And voilà! The chocolate is ready for chefs to confect all manner of exquisite delights.

I will apply the techniques I have used in teaching and coaching professional pastry chefs, chocolate makers, and apprentices over the years to simplify your understanding of the use of chocolate and to help you create all the confections in this book like a professional chef.

The Difference between Good Chocolate and Imitation (Compound) Chocolate

Good quality chocolate must contain cocoa solids, cocoa butter, sugar, vanilla, and lecithin. It's known as *couverture*.

According to the Health and Welfare of Canada, the following standards must apply:

Dark chocolate must contain a minimum of 30–35 percent cocoa components and 18 percent cocoa butter. The flavor profile should be a cocoa taste that is fruity, bitter, spicy, and sometimes nutty, depending on the origin of the beans used.

Milk chocolate must contain a minimum of 25 percent milk fat. The characteristic taste of milk chocolate is smooth, milky, nutty, and caramel flavored.

White chocolate must contain a minimum of 20 percent cocoa butter and 12–14 percent milk components. The taste is qualified as creamy, sweet, and milky.

To achieve good chocolate couverture, you need to pre-crystallise. However, you do not need to pre-crystallise compound chocolate (Pâte a glacer or imitations). This is inexpensive chocolate that typically uses hydrogenated fat, palm kernel oil, or coconut oil instead of cocoa butter. Hydrogenated fat is known to be very bad for people's health.

When you achieve pre-crystallisation with couverture chocolate, you can create beautiful chocolate show-pieces, shiny molded bonbons, etc.

Tempering or Pre-crystallisation?

When you hear about tempering and pre-crystallisation from a chef, the processes seem complicated and difficult to achieve. I would like to clear up any misconceptions; to do so, I will explain the difference between tempering and crystallisation. The goal is to create a stable structure of fat crystals within a precise temperature zone. When you achieve tempering and control it, you will be able to do any chocolate work, such as dipping a strawberry and having it set at room temperature rather than in the fridge and also having your chocolate set with a shine like that of the beautiful bonbons in a professional chocolate shop.

First let us take a look at dairy butter.

When butter is heated, it melts to a liquid state. And when it cools down, it will return to solid. This happens because butter is fat, which is structured into what we call *crystals*. These crystals are very sensitive to temperature fluctuations.

So which is the right term, *tempering* or *pre-crystallisation?*

Overall, good chocolates react in the same way. However there are several types of fat crystals in chocolate. The key is to create and line up the correct fat crystal at the correct temperature in order to make the fat structure stable. Because the goal is to *create and line up the right crystals,* the term *tempering* does not apply. For centuries, we though temperature was doing all the work; that's why we called it tempering. We now know this is not the case, so the correct term is *pre-crystallisation.* When you have good pre-crystallisation, your chocolate should be shiny and resistant to heat, and it should also give you a good snap.

For pre-crystallisation to occur, three factors must be controlled: temperature, time, and (most important) movement.

Pre-crystallisation:

Method#1: Stovetop melting of callet or pistole (these are small, flat chocolate chips)

For Dark Couverture Chocolate

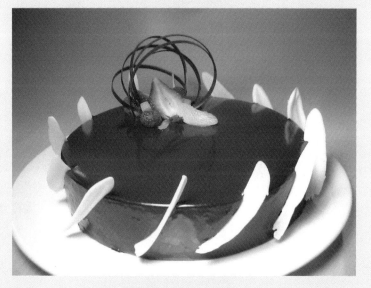

We need to melt 1 kg (2.2 lbs) of chocolate to 45°C (113°F) and keep it at this temperature for a minimum of ten minutes to ensure all unstable crystals are melted. Then add in 200–250 g (1½ cups–1¾ cups) of pistole or callet and stir well until completely melted. The temperature should be 32°C (90°F) after the addition. Dip one side of a 2″ × 3″ piece of parchment paper into the chocolate. The chocolate should harden in three to five minutes. The chocolate should harden evenly and have a smooth surface without any fat lines or traces of crystals. After seven minutes, it should snap when bent. Your chocolate is now pre-crystallised and ready to use for dipping or molding.

Keep the bowl of chocolate on a double boiler filled with *just hot water from the tap*, and change the water every ten minutes to keep the temperature at 32°C (90°F). You may alternatively use a hair dryer to maintain the temperature; however, do not heat the chocolate for too long, as you might melt all the crystals, requiring that you perform the pre-crystallisation again.

For Milk Chocolate and White Chocolate

When working with milk chocolate or white chocolate, the pre-crystallisation temperatures are slightly different.

Melt 1 kg (2.2 lbs) of chocolate at 45°C (113°F). Add 200–250 g (1½ cups to 1¾ cups) of pistole or callet and stir well until completed melted. Bring the chocolate to 30°C (86°F) for milk couverture and 29°C (84°F) for white chocolate, and then maintain the temperature as for dark couverture on a double boiler for dipping or molding.

Method #2: Microwave

To slowly melt the chocolate in a microwave, heat the chocolate for intervals of thirty seconds, stirring after each interval, until the chocolate is halfway melted. Then reduce the interval time to five seconds. Ensure a good stirring every time before you place the chocolate back in the microwave. Once the chocolate has reached its working temperature 32°C (90°F) for dark couverture, 30°C (86°F) for milk couverture, and 29°C (84°F) for white chocolate, maintain the temperature on a double boiler and use it for the needed application.

*Paper tests are required to ensure you have a good pre-crystallisation for all techniques and chocolates.

What is Ganache?

Ganache is an emulsion of the fat in its ingredients and its water content. The fat is dairy fat and cocoa butter fat. The water is from dairy products, such as cream, milk, or dairy butter. To achieve an exquisite taste and texture, we need to emulsify the ganache well at a warm temperature.

When knowledgeable chefs make truffles by boiling cream or milk with chocolate, they ask us to place the ganache in a fridge to set. Sometimes your ganache may separate and you may not know why. Conclusion: major heat, major problem.

When you make a ganache with just enough heat to melt your chocolate, you will emulsify your ingredients and it will set at room temperature in about one hour. It will also give you a smooth end product with a low melting point that provides an explosion of flavor in your mouth.

To help us achieve the emulsification, we will use a food processor. The technique is simple.

For dark couverture, heat the liquid to 70°C (158°F).
For milk couverture, heat the liquid to 65°C (149°F).
For white chocolate, heat the liquid to 60°C (140°F).

Place the chocolate couverture (in pistole or callet form) in a food processor. Heat the cream and or milk, butter, and sugar (glucose or corn syrup) to the desired temperature. Pour the hot liquid over the chocolate and turn on the food processor to emulsify the ganache.

If you would like to make all your recipes like a pro, it is highly recommend that you _weigh out all ingredients in metric units_, as doing so is much more accurate than using imperial measuring for baking and making pastries.

Making Chocolate Shells with a Polycarbonate Mold

Hold the polycarbonate mold in one hand, and with the other hand use a spatula to bring the chocolate over the mold and fill the opening. Tap on the side of the mold to bring any bubbles to the surface, and then flip the mold upside down. Lightly tap on the bottom to remove the extra chocolate and create a hollow shell. Use a scraper to clean up the side of the mold, and then place the mold upside down on a sheet of parchment paper for five minutes. When the chocolate is well pre-crystallised, it will set in three minutes. Allow the chocolate shell to set for thirty minutes before filling with ganache.

Filling with Ganache

Using a piping bag, lightly squeeze the ganache into the shell, filling to ¾ of the way to the top. Allow it to set at room temperature. It may take from one to six hours to set.

Capping the shells

Use a ladle to pour a thin coat of pre-crystallised chocolate over the opening. Using a plastic scraper, scrape away the excess chocolate from right to left, and repeat the step from left to right to seal the ganache in the shell.

You should work as cleanly as possible to prevent chocolate ending up all over your working area. Remember, the chocolate is not messy; it is just we who put it everywhere.

After every use, wash your chocolate molds in lukewarm water and soap. Dry them right away to prevent the chlorine in the city water from damaging them. The presence of chlorine residue will etch your mold and prevent your chocolate from coming out shiny.

Before every use, remember to polish your mold with a cotton ball; this will help ensure your chocolate will be shiny.

Dipping a Ganache

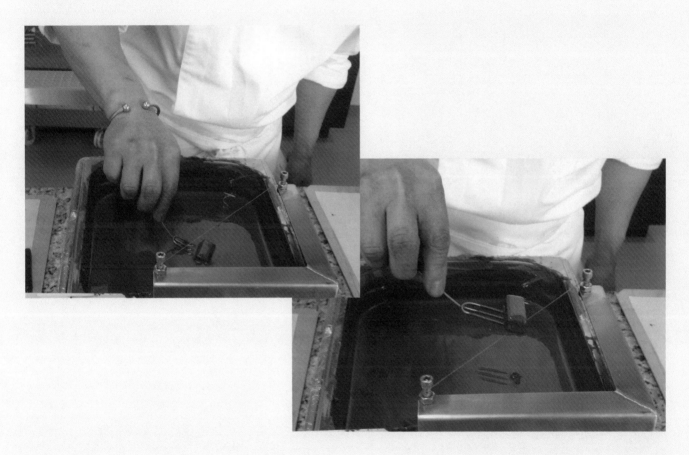

Before dipping the ganache, ensure that the ganache is free of debris, and then dip it into pre-crystallised chocolate. Clean any excess chocolate from the bottom of the bonbon by scraping against the rim of the bowl or the melting vessel.

Truffles

Armagnac Truffles

Yield: 60–75 pieces
Preparation time: one hour

Ingredients:
500 g (3⅓ cups) 70% dark chocolate in pistole form or chopped into small pieces
300 ml (1⅓ cups) 35% cream
80 g (3 tbsp) corn syrup
150 g (2⅓ cups) unsalted butter
80 g (3 tbsp) Armagnac liquor

Place the dark chocolate couverture in a food processor.

In a saucepan, heat cream, corn syrup, and butter to 70°C (158°F). Pour over the dark chocolate couverture and mix in the food processor until a smooth emulsion is obtained. Add Armagnac and mix well. Let set in a bowl at room temperature, and then scoop or pipe into a melon ball shape.

Let cool at room temperature for a minimum of two hours.

Dip each piece in pre-crystallised dark chocolate couverture and roll in cocoa powder. Keep each piece in the cacao powder for ten minutes before removal.

Bonbons can be kept at room temperature for one week.

Tips: Substitute Armagnac with rum, whiskey, etc., or leave alcohol out altogether. Never keep truffles or bonbons in the refrigerator. Use red cocoa powder for taste and appearance.

Jamaican Truffles

Yield: 50–60 pieces
Preparation time: one hour

Ingredients:
175 ml (½ cup) 35% cream
40 g (2 tbsp) corn syrup
50 g (¼ cup) unsalted butter
700 g (5¼ cups) 60% dark chocolate, in pistole form or chopped into small pieces
30 g (2 tbsp) Jamaican rum
3 vanilla beans (split open lengthwise; use only the seeds)

Place the dark chocolate couverture in a food processor.

In a saucepan, heat cream, corn syrup, butter, and vanilla beans to 70°C (158°F). Pour over the dark chocolate couverture and mix in the food processor until a smooth emulsion is obtained. Add rum and mix well.

Let set in chocolate frame or baking tray overnight. Cut into 2.5 cm × 1 cm pieces.

When set, dip the pieces into pre-crystallised dark chocolate couverture. Before the chocolate sets, place a straw on top to create a decorative pattern. Let the chocolate set for one hour before removing the straw.

Bonbons can be kept at room temperature for one week.

Tip: Fill chocolate shells with Jamaican ganache. Let them set for a couple of hours before sealing the openings with pre-crystallised dark chocolate couverture.

Port Wine Truffles

Yield: 55–65 pieces
Preparation time: one hour

Ingredients:
600 g 4 cups, 60% dark chocolate in pistole forms or chops into small pieces
360 g (1½ cups) ruby port
180 g (¾ cup) 35% cream
70 g (⅓ cup) unsalted butter
65 g (4 tbsp) corn syrup

Place the dark chocolate couverture in a food processor.

In a saucepan, heat cream, ruby port, butter, and corn syrup to 70°C (158°F). Pour over the dark chocolate couverture and mix in the food processor until a smooth emulsion is obtained. Let set in a bowl at room temperature.

Fill dark chocolate shells with ganache. Let set for couple hours before sealing the opening with pre-crystallised dark chocolate couverture.

Bonbons can be kept at room temperature for one week.

Tip: You can substitute ruby port with Bailey's, Banyuls, or Maury.

Kappuccino

Yield: 55–60 pieces
Preparation time: one hour

Ingredients:
150 ml (1½ cups) 35% cream
375 g (2¾ cups) milk chocolate in pistole form or chopped into small pieces
30 g (2 tbsp) honey
180 g (¾ cup) unsalted butter
30 g (2 tbsp) espresso

Place the milk chocolate couverture in a food processor.

In a saucepan, heat cream, honey, butter, and espresso to 65°C (149°F). Pour over the milk chocolate couverture and mix in the food processor until a smooth emulsion is obtained. Let set in a bowl at room temperature.

Fill milk chocolate shells with ganache.

Let set at room temperature for two hours before sealing the opening with pre-crystallised milk chocolate couverture.

Alternatively confectionary frame with ganache and allow to set overnight. Cut into squares and dip in pre-crystallised milk chocolate couverture.

Bonbons can be kept at room temperature for one week.

Tip: For decorations, mix gold dust with a small amount of vodka or rum and use a clean sponge to stamp the gold dust on the chocolate.

Chocolate Caramel

Yield 40–50 pieces
Preparation time: one hour

Ingredients:
500 g (3 cups) sugar
250 g (1 cup) 35% cream
250 g (1 cup) clear corn syrup
50 g (4 tbsp) unsalted butter
50 g (½ cup) semisweet dark chocolate in pistole form or chopped into small pieces

In a saucepan, combine sugar, cream, and corn syrup and bring to a boil. Cook until it reaches 110°C (232°F).

Add butter and chocolate; cook until it reaches 118°C–123°C (244°F–253°F).

Pour over Silpat (silicone baking mat) in a chocolate frame or a lightly oiled baking tray to prevent from sticking.

Let cool and cut into 1.5 cm × 1.5 cm pieces. Dip in pre-crystallised milk chocolate or dark chocolate couverture.

Bonbons can be kept at room temperature for one week.

Honey Chardon

Yield: 60–75 pieces
Preparation time: one hour

Ingredients:
125 ml (½ cup) 35% cream
120 g (½ cup) unsalted butter
300 g (1⅓ cups) honey
700 g (4¾ cups) milk chocolate in pistole forms or chopped into small pieces

Place the milk chocolate couverture in a food processor.

In a saucepan, combine cream, butter, and honey and heat to 65°C (149°F). Pour over milk chocolate couverture and mix in the food processor until a smooth emulsion is obtained. Let set in a bowl at room temperature. Scoop or pipe into melon ball shape. Let set for two hours.

Dip the truffles into pre-crystallised milk chocolate couverture and lay over a baking grill immediately.

Wait until chocolate starts to set, and then use a fork to quickly roll the truffles over the grill to create the desired texture.

Bonbons can be kept at room temperature for one week.

Tip: The less you roll the chardon on the grill, the shinier it becomes.

Lavender Truffles

Yield: 50–60 pieces
Preparation time: one hour

Ingredients:
300 g (2 cups) 70% dark chocolate in pistole form or chopped into small pieces
250 g (1 cup) 35% cream
40 g (2 tbsp) honey
50 g (2½ tbsp) unsalted butter
2 g (½ tsp) dry lavender flowers

Place the dark chocolate couverture in a food processor.

In a saucepan, combine cream, honey, butter, and lavender and heat to 90°C (194°F). Let the lavender infuse for ten minutes.

Drain the flowers and heat the mixture to 70°C (158°F). Pour over dark chocolate couverture and mix in the food processor until a smooth emulsion is obtained. Let set in a bowl at room temperature.

Fill milk chocolate shells with ganache.

Let set for two to three hours before sealing the opening with pre-crystallised milk chocolate couverture.

Bonbons can be kept at room temperature for one week.

Tip: Do not infuse the lavender for too long; otherwise, the chocolate will have a soapy taste.

Carré d'Orange

Yield: 50–60 pieces
Preparation time: one hour

Ingredients:
225 g (1½ cups) 64% dark chocolate in pistole form or chopped into small pieces
300 g (2 cups) milk chocolate in pistole form or chopped into small pieces
300 g (1⅓ cups) 35% cream
50 g (2½ tbsp) unsalted butter
Orange oil to taste

Place the dark chocolate and milk chocolate couvertures in a food processor.

In a saucepan, combine cream and butter and heat to 70°C (149°F). Pour over chocolate couvertures and make a smooth emulsion. Add orange oil to taste.

Spread out in a chocolate frame and cut into 1.5 cm × 1.5 cm pieces. Dip pieces into pre-crystallised dark chocolate couverture. Decorate with small pieces of textured plastic or acetate on top. Let set for forty-five minutes, and then peel off the plastic or acetate.

Bonbons can be kept at room temperature for one week.

Mendiant

Preparation time: thirty minutes

Ingredients:
Semisweet chocolate as needed
Dried fruits and nuts as needed

Pre-crystallise the chocolate couverture. Using a piping bag, pipe 4 cm (1½") discs on baking paper. Place a few pieces of dried fruits and nuts on each disc before the chocolate sets up.

Bonbons can be kept at room temperature for one week.

Tips: Use dried cranberries, golden raisins, small pieces of apricot, pistachios, almonds, and walnuts. Make sure you have colorful mendiants for display purposes or gifts. Do not make too many chocolate discs at the same time; only the number you can handle.

Earl Grey

Yield: 40–60 pieces
Preparation time: 1 hour

Ingredients:
250 g (1⅔ cups) milk chocolate in pistole form or chopped into small pieces
200 g (¾ cup) 35% cream
10 g (8 bags) Earl Grey tea
40 g (2½ tbsp) honey
40 g (2½ tbsp) unsalted butter

Place the milk chocolate couverture in a food processor.

In a saucepan, combine cream and butter and heat to 90°C (194°F). Add tea bags and allow to infuse for five minutes.

Drain all tea bags, add honey, and heat to 70°C (158°F). Pour over milk chocolate couverture and mix in the food processor until a smooth emulsion is obtained.

Spread out in a chocolate frame or a cake pan lined with baking paper or acetate. Let set overnight. Cut into 1.5 cm × 1.5 cm pieces. Dip pieces in tempered milk chocolate.

Alternatively, fill chocolate shells with ganache and let set for three to four hours before sealing the opening with pre-crystallised milk chocolate couverture.

Bonbons can be kept at room temperature for one week.

Tip: Do not infuse tea in boiling cream or water, and do not infuse for longer than five minutes. Otherwise, it will bring out the bitterness of the tea rather than its flavor.

Lemonada

Yield: 50–60 pieces
Preparation time: one hour

Ingredients:
375 g (2¾ cups) white chocolate in pistole form or chopped into small pieces
3 lemon zest
80 g (5 tbsp) fresh lemon juice
4 egg yolks
50 g (3 tbsp) sugar
80 g (4 tbsp) unsalted butter

Place the white chocolate couverture in a food processor.

Combine egg yolks and sugar and whisk to ribbon stage.

In a saucepan, combine lemon juice and lemon zest and bring to a boil. Pour into yolk mixture and heat to 90°C (194°F). Add butter. Pour over the white chocolate couverture and mix in the food processor until a smooth emulsion is obtained. Let the ganache cool at room temperature.

In the meantime, prepare the white chocolate shells. Fill the white chocolate shells with ganache and let set at room temperature for three to four hours before sealing the opening with pre-crystallised white chocolate couverture.

Bonbons can be kept at room temperature for one week.

Tip: You can replace the lemon products with any kind of citrus fruits or a combination of them.

Chocolate Drinks
& Fondue

Mexicana Hot Chocolate

Yield: 6 cups
Preparation time: twenty minutes

Ingredients:
1 L (4 cups) water
125 ml (½ cup) 35% cream
150 g (1½ cups) cocoa powder
Cinnamon to taste
Star anise to taste
Nutmeg to taste
100 g (½ cup) sugar
3 orange slices

In a saucepan, combine water, cream, sugar, and cocoa powder and bring to a boil.

Use an electric hand blender to mix thoroughly.

Add all the spices and orange slices and allow to infuse for five to ten minutes.

Serve hot with a touch of whipped cream or cappuccino foam.

Four-Spice Hot Chocolate

Yield: 6 cups
Preparation time: twenty minutes

Ingredients:
1 L (4 cups) 3.25% milk
200 g (1½ cups) 70% dark chocolate seeds
1 pinch cinnamon
1 pinch nutmeg
1 pinch star anise
4 slices fresh ginger
1 vanilla bean (split open lengthwise; use only the seeds)

In a saucepan, combine all ingredients. Use an electric hand blender to mix while the mixture is heating up.

Serve hot with a touch of whipped cream, marshmallows, or cappuccino foam.

Tip: To make chocolate seeds, place small pieces of chocolate in a food processor and chop until small seeds are obtained. Do not over mix; otherwise, chocolate will become a paste and might not melt.

Hot Chocolate Sip

Yield: 6 cups
Preparation time: twenty minutes

Ingredients:
1 L (4 cups) 3.25% milk
200 g (¾ cup) 35% cream
300 g (2 cups) Belgian bittersweet chocolate in pistole form or chopped into small pieces
100 g (½ cup) sugar
2 g (2 pinches) cinnamon
1 g (1 pinch) nutmeg
2 vanilla beans (split open lengthwise; use only the seeds)

In a saucepan, combine milk, cream, chocolate, sugar, cinnamon, nutmeg, and vanilla seeds and bring to a boil. Use an electric hand blender to mix.

Serve hot with a touch of whipped cream, marshmallows, or cappuccino foam.

Spicy Honey Hot Chocolate

Yield: 6 cups
Preparation time: twenty minutes

Ingredients:
1 L (4 cups) 3.25% milk
200 g (¾ cup) 35% cream
200 g (1½ cups), 70% dark chocolate in pistole form or chopped into small pieces
50 g (4 tbsp) sugar
80 g (6 tbsp) honey
1 pinch cinnamon
1 pinch nutmeg

In a saucepan, combine all ingredients and bring to a boil; use an electric hand blender to mix.

Serve cold or hot with a touch of whipped cream or cappuccino foam.

Tip: All hot drinks can be served with biscotti or chocolate cookies.

Chocolate Milkshake

Yield: 4 jumbo milkshakes
Preparation time: thirty minutes

Ingredients:
500 g (2 cups) 3.25% milk
60 g (4 tbsp) 35% cream
150 g (1 cup) Belgian bittersweet chocolate in pistole form or chopped into small pieces
15 g (1 tbsp) lemon zest
8 scoops ice cream, any flavor

In a saucepan, combine milk, cream, chocolate, and lemon zest and bring to a boil. Use an electric hand blender to mix thoroughly. Place in refrigerator.

For each shake, blend 2 scoops of ice cream with 250 g (1 cup) of the chocolate base in an electric blender.

Tip: A couple drops of essential oil may be added for flavor. Such as: ylang-ylang, lavender, lemon, rose petals, instant coffee, etc.

Martini Chocolate Shake

Yield: 6 shakes
Preparation time: thirty minutes

Ingredients:
250 g (1 cup) 3.25% milk
250 g (1 cup) 35% cream
175 g (1¼ cups) Belgian dark chocolate in pistole form or chopped into small pieces
5 g (1 tsp) lemon zest
10 g (2 tsp) orange zest
Liquor of your choice

In a saucepan, combine all ingredients and bring to a boil. Use an electric hand blender to mix thoroughly. Place in the refrigerator.

In a shaker, add 125 g (½ cup) of the chocolate mixture, liquor to taste, and ice cubes. Shake well, pour into cocktail glasses, and serve cold.

Tip: Use Kahlua, rum, Grand Marnier, Bailey's, Armagnac, cassis, etc.

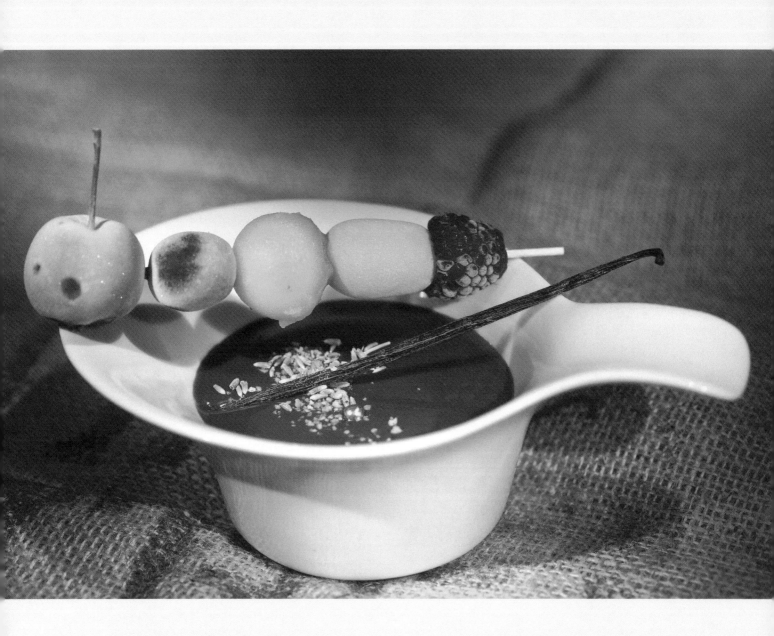

Chocolate Fondue

Yield: 6 portions
Preparation time: thirty minutes

Ingredients:
250 g (1 cup) 35% cream
180 g (¾ cup) half-and-half cream
30 g (2 tbsp) unsalted butter
80 g (5 tbsp) corn syrup
675 g (5¼ cups) milk chocolate in pistole form or chopped into small pieces
25 g (1 oz) Cointreau

In a saucepan, combine cream, half-and-half cream, butter, and corn syrup and bring to a boil. Pour the hot liquid over the chocolate couverture and allow it to melt. Use an electric hand blender to mix thoroughly. Pour into a fondue pot and maintain temperature at 50°C (122°F).

Dip small fruits, lady fingers, and small sponge cakes into fondue and serve.

Fondue can be refrigerated for one week; reheat as needed.

Tip: You may use other liquors, such as Bailey's, Cointreau, raspberry liquor, or maple cream.

Duocolaté Fondue

Yield: 6 portions
Preparation time: thirty minutes

Ingredients:
250 g (1 cup) 3.25% milk
180 g (¾ cup) 35% cream
50 g (3½ tbsp) honey
1 lemon zest
1 orange zest
3 g (1 pinch) ground cinnamon
600 g (4 cups) 70% dark chocolate in pistole form or chopped into small pieces
100 g (¾ cup) milk chocolate in pistole form or chopped into small pieces
30 g (1 oz) liquor (Grand Marnier, Bailey's, raspberry liquor, etc.)

In a saucepan, combine cream, milk, honey, orange zest, lemon zest, and cinnamon and bring to a boil. Pour over the chocolate couvertures and liquor and allow to melt. Use an electric hand blender to mix thoroughly. Pour into a fondue pot and maintain temperature at 50°C (122°F).

Dip small fruits, lady fingers, and small sponge cakes into fondue and serve.

Fondue can be refrigerated for one week; reheat as needed.

Tip: Spices may be added for flavor.

White Chocolate and Peanut Butter Fondue

Yield: 6 portions
Preparation time: thirty minutes

Ingredients:
180 g (¾ cup) 3.25% milk
180 g (¾ cup) 35% cream
60 g (4 tbsp) corn syrup
150 g (½ cup) natural peanut butter
500 g (3½ cups) white chocolate in pistole form or chopped into small pieces
50 g (1¾ oz) Kahlua liquor

In a large bowl, combine the peanut butter and chocolate couverture.

In a saucepan, combine milk, cream, and corn syrup and bring to a boil. Pour the cream mixture into the peanut butter and chocolate couverture mixture. Use an electric hand blender to mix thoroughly. Add the Kahlua. Pour into a fondue pot and maintain temperature at 50°C (122°F).

Dip small fruits, lady fingers, and small sponge cakes into fondue and serve.

Fondue can be refrigerated for one week; reheat as needed.

Tip: Instant coffee or espresso may be added for flavor.

White Chocolate Canadian Maple Fondue

Yield: 6 portions
Preparation time: thirty minutes

Ingredients:
250 g (1 cup) 3.25% milk
180 g (¾ cup) 35% cream
100 g (½ cup) maple syrup
700 g (4¾ cups) white chocolate in pistole form or chopped into small pieces
100 g (½ cup) unsalted butter

In a saucepan, combine milk, cream, and maple syrup and bring to a boil. Pour over the chocolate and allow it to melt. Add butter. Use an electric hand blender to mix thoroughly. Pour into a fondue pot and serve at 50°C (122°F).

Dip small fruits, lady fingers, and small sponge cakes into fondue and serve.

Fondue can be refrigerated for one week; reheat as needed.

Cookies

Chocolate Chip Cookies

Yield: 2 dozens
Preparation time: forty-five minutes

Ingredients:
170 g (1½ cups) all-purpose flour
170 g (1½ cups) cake flour
5 g (1 tsp) baking soda
7 g (1 tsp) salt
175 g (1 cup) sugar
175 g (1 cup) brown sugar
225 g (1 cup) butter
2 ml (3 drops) vanilla extract
2 large eggs
300 g (2 cups) 70% dark chocolate in pistole form or chopped into small pieces

Preheat oven to 163°C (325°F).

In a mixing bowl, sift together flour, baking soda, and salt.

In a mixer, cream together sugar and butter. Add eggs one at a time, mixing until fluffy. Fold in flour, baking soda, and salt by hand to form dough. Add dark chocolate.

Shape into pieces about the size of a ping-pong ball. Place on a baking tray lined with parchment paper.

Bake at 163°C (325°F) for fifteen to twenty minutes.

Cookies can be stored in cookie jar for three days.

White Chocolate Pecan Cookies

Yield: 4 dozens
Preparation time: forty-five minutes

Ingredients:
200 g (1⅓ cups) sugar
435 g (2 cups) brown sugar
330 g (1⅓ cups) unsalted butter
4 large eggs
30 ml (1 tsp) vanilla extract
675 g (6¾ cups) all-purpose flour
6 g (1 tsp) baking soda
3 g (½ tsp) salt
235 g (1½ cups) chopped pecan
400 g (3 cups) white chocolate chips in pistole form or chopped into small pieces

Preheat oven to 163°C (325°F).

In a mixing bowl, sift together flour, baking soda, and salt.

In a mixer, cream together sugar and butter. Add eggs one at a time. Mix until fluffy. Fold in flour, baking soda, and salt by hand to form dough. Add pecans and chocolate chips.

Shape into pieces about the size of a ping-pong ball. Place on a baking tray lined with parchment paper.

Bake at 163°C (325°F) for fifteen to twenty minutes.

Cookies can be stored in cookie jar for three days.

Double Chocolate Pecan Cookies

Yield 4 dozens
Preparation time: forty-five minutes

Ingredients:
445 g (1¾ cups) unsalted butter
230 g (1¼ cups) brown sugar
185 g (1 cup) sugar
80 g (7 tbsp) corn syrup
4 large eggs
30 g (2 tbsp) vanilla extract
400 g (4 cups) pastry flour
3 g (1 pinch) salt
7 g (1¼ tsp) baking soda
150 g (1½ cups) cocoa powder
115 g (1 cup) crushed pecans
160 g (1¼ cups) chocolate chips

Preheat oven to 155°C (311°F).

In a mixing bowl, sift together flour, baking soda, cocoa powder, and salt.

In a mixer, cream together butter, sugar, brown sugar, and corn syrup. Add eggs one at a time. Fold in flour, baking soda, cocoa powder, and salt by hand to form dough. Add vanilla, chocolate chips, and pecans.

Shape into pieces about the size of a ping-pong ball. Place on a baking tray lined with parchment paper.

Bake in the oven at 155°C (311°F) for eighteen to twenty minutes.

Cookies can be stored in cookie jar for three days.

Chocolate Brownie Cookies

Yield: 2 dozens
Preparation time: thirty minutes

Ingredients:
250 g (1⅔ cups) 65% dark chocolate in pistole form or chopped into small pieces
90 g (⅓ cup) unsalted butter
2 large eggs
200 g (1 cup) brown sugar
5 ml (1 tsp) vanilla extract
150 g (1½ cups) pastry flour
2.5 g (½ tsp) baking powder
2.5 g (½ tsp) Maldon salt

Preheat oven to 177°C (350°F).

In a plastic bowl, combine chocolate and butter. Melt in microwave or over a double boiler.

In a mixer, cream brown sugar, eggs, and vanilla for one minute. Add the melted chocolate and butter mixture into the egg mixture and mix for another minute. Using a spatula, fold by hand the flour, baking powder, and salt into the chocolate mixture.

Allow the mixture to sit for one hour at room temperature. Scoop into pieces about the size of a ping-pong ball and place them 2" apart on a baking tray lined with parchment paper.

Bake for seven minutes at 177°C (350°F).

Remove from oven and sprinkle with icing sugar. Let cool on the tray and serve.

Cookies can be stored in cookie jar for three days.

Tip: Do not bake cookies ahead of time; they will become very hard.

Triple Chocolate Chip Cookies

Yield: 4 dozens
Preparation time: forty-five minutes

Ingredients:
265 g (1¼ cups) unsalted butter
185 g (1 cup) sugar
185 g (1 cup) brown sugar
6 ml (1 tsp) vanilla extract
3 large eggs
350 g (3½ cups) all-purpose flour
3 g (3 pinches) baking soda
4 g (4 pinches) sea salt
185 g (1¼ cups) 60% dark chocolate in pistole form or chopped into small pieces
135 g (1 cup) milk chocolate in pistole form or chopped into small pieces
135 g (1 cup) white chocolate in pistole form or chopped into small pieces
160 g (1½ cups) pecan pieces

Preheat oven to 155°C (311°F).

In a mixing bowl, sift together flour, baking soda, and salt.

In a mixer, cream together butter, sugar, and brown sugar. Add eggs one at a time. Fold in flour, baking soda, and salt by hand to form dough. Add vanilla, the three types of chocolate, and pecans. Do not overwork the mixture.

Shape into pieces about the size of a ping-pong ball. Place on a baking tray lined with parchment paper.

Bake in the oven at 155°C (311°F) for eighteen to twenty minutes.

Cookies can be stored in cookie jar for three days.

Tip: Dried cranberries, raisins, other types of nuts, or other types of chocolate may be substituted.

Pâtisserie et Dessert

Chocolate Almond Biscotti

Yield 2 logs (2 dozens)
Preparation time: forty-five minutes

Ingredients:

220 g (2¼ cups) all-purpose flour	2 large eggs
225 g (1 cup) sugar	2 egg whites
40 g (3 tbsp) cocoa powder	5 ml (1 tsp) vanilla extract
5 g (1 tsp) baking soda	75 g (½ cup) toasted whole almonds
1 pinch salt	70 g (½ cup) chocolate chips

Preheat oven to 163°C (325°F).

Line two large baking sheets with parchment paper (or use nonstick baking sheets).

In a stainless steel bowl, mix together eggs, egg whites, and vanilla extract.

In a mixer with a paddle attachment, combine flour, sugar, cocoa powder, baking soda, and salt. Mixing at low speed, gradually add the egg mixture to the flour mixture. Combine almonds and chocolate chips, and then add to the flour mixture and blend just until combined.

Sprinkle work surface with all-purpose flour. Roll dough into two logs that are 2 inch in diameter.

Place logs on baking sheet lined with parchment paper (or use nonstick baking sheets) and brush with beaten egg. Bake at 177°C (350°F) until light golden brown, about thirty to thirty-five minutes.

Allow logs to cool for fifteen minutes and then cut into slices on the bias. Place slices on greased sheet pan or baking paper and bake at 177°C (350°F) for about ten to fifteen minutes until toasted.

Let cool and store in an airtight container.

Biscotti can be stored in cookie jar for two weeks.

Tip: Almond slices or any kind of nuts may be substituted for whole almonds. Biscotti can be dipped into pre-crystallised milk chocolate or dark chocolate couverture.

Chocolate Biscotti

Yield: 2 logs (2 dozens)
Preparation time: forty-five minutes

Ingredients:

330 g (3¼ cups) all-purpose flour	4 large eggs
60 g (4 tbsp) cocoa powder	1 lemon zest
10 g (2 tsp) baking powder	10 ml (2 tsp) coffee liquor
170 g (¾ cup) unsalted butter	90 g (¾ cup) 70% dark chocolate chunks
180 g (1 cup) granulated sugar	80 g (1 cup) whole blanched almonds, toasted

Preheat oven to 163°C (325°F).

Line two large baking sheets with parchment paper (or use nonstick baking sheets).

In a large bowl, sift together flour, cocoa powder, baking powder, and salt.

In a mixer with a paddle attachment, cream together butter and sugar. Mix until light and fluffy. Add eggs, one at a time. Add lemon zest and liquor. At low speed, add the flour mixture and blend just until combined. Fold in by hand chocolate chunks and almonds.

Sprinkle work surface with all-purpose flour. Divide dough in half. Roll each piece into a 15 inch long log. Arrange the logs 3 inch apart on a prepared baking sheet.

Bake for thirty minutes or until the center of each log is firm when gently pressed with fingertip.

Allow logs to cool fifteen minutes and then slice each log crosswise into ¼ inch thick slices. Place slices on a greased sheet pan or baking paper and bake at 177°C (350°F) for about ten to fifteen minutes until toasted.

Let cool and store in an airtight container.

Biscotti can be stored in cookie jar for two weeks.

Tip: Dried fruits or salty bacon may be added.

Chocolate Pistachio Biscotti

Yield: 2 logs (2 dozens)
Preparation time: forty-five minutes

Ingredients:
110 g (½ cup) unsalted butter
340 g (1¾ cups) granulated sugar
6 large eggs
20 ml (2 tbsp) orange juice
500 g (5 cups) unbleached organic flour

170 g (1½ cups) cocoa powder
20 g (4 tsp) baking powder
10 g (2 tsp) baking soda
120 g (1½ cups) pistachio nuts, chopped (raw or toasted)
100 g (¾ cup) chocolate chips

Preheat oven to 163°C (325°F).

Line a large baking sheet with parchment paper or use nonstick baking sheets.

In a large bowl, sift together flour, cocoa powder, baking powder, and baking soda.

In a mixer with a paddle attachment, cream together butter and sugar. Mix until light and fluffy. Add eggs, one at a time. Add orange juice. At low speed, mix in flour mixture and blend just until combined. Fold in by hand chocolate chunks and pistachios.

Sprinkle work surface with all-purpose flour. Divide dough in half. Roll each piece into a 15 inch long log. Arrange the logs 3 inch apart on a prepared baking sheet. Bake for thirty minutes or until the centers of the logs are firm when gently pressed with a fingertip.

Allow to cool for fifteen minutes and then slice crosswise into slices that are from ¼ inch thick slices. Place slices on a greased sheet pan or baking paper and bake at 177°C (350°F) for about ten to fifteen minutes until toasted.

Let cool and store in an airtight container.

Biscotti can be stored in cookie jar for two weeks.

Banana Chocolate Chip Muffins

Yield: 12 large muffins
Preparation time: forty-five minutes

Ingredients:
225 g (1 cup) white sugar
180 ml (¾ cup) vegetable oil
2 large eggs
115 g (1 cup) bananas
45 g (3 tbsp) sour cream
5 g (1 tsp) baking soda
220 g (2¼ cups) all-purpose flour
80 g (¾ cup) chocolate chips

Preheat oven to 200°C (400°F).

Line muffin pan with muffin cups, or use a silicone muffin pan.

In a mixer with a paddle attachment, combine sugar and oil and add eggs and then bananas. Beat thoroughly at low speed. Slowly add sour cream to banana mixture. Sift in flour and baking soda. Stir gently until just blended. Add chocolate chips.

Fill muffins cups ¾ of the way to the top. Bake for twenty to twenty-five minutes.

Let muffins cool for five minutes and then remove from pans and cool on rack.

Muffins can be kept at room temperature for two days.

Tip: You may vary the recipe by using walnuts, almonds, or dried or fresh fruits.

Coffee Walnut Chocolate Chip Muffins

Yield: 12 large muffins
Preparation time: forty-five minutes

Ingredients:
110 ml (½ cup) vegetable oil
115 g (½ cup) brown sugar
115 g (½ cup) white sugar
45 g (2½ tbsp) instant coffee
10 ml (2 tsp) vanilla extract
2 large eggs
158 g (¾ cup) 3.25% milk
200 g (2 cups) flour
3 pinches salt
10 g (2 tsp) baking powder
80 g (¾ cup) semi-sweet chocolate chips
120 g (1½ cups) walnuts, coarsely chopped

Preheat oven to 177°C (350°F).

Line muffin pan with muffin cups or use a silicone muffin pan.

Dissolve the instant coffee in vanilla extract.

In a mixer with a paddle attachment, combine oil, sugars, coffee, and vanilla. Beat together the eggs and milk. With mixer at low speed, sift in flour, salt, and baking powder. Gently stir until just blended. Add chocolate chips and walnuts.

Fill muffins cups ¾ of the way to the top. Bake for twenty to twenty-five minutes or until a toothpick inserted in the center comes out clean.

Let muffins cool for five minutes and then remove from pans and cool on rack.

Muffins can be kept at room temperature for two days.

White Chocolate Chip Macadamia Nut Muffins

Yield: 24 medium muffins
Preparation time: forty-five minutes

Streusel

Ingredients:
30 g (3 tbsp) all-purpose flour
70 g (6½ tbsp) brown sugar
30 g (2 tbsp) butter

In a mixer with a paddle attachment, combine flour and brown sugar and blend well. Add butter and mix until the mixture resembles coarse crumbs. Set aside.

Muffins

Ingredients:
220 g (2¼ cups) flour
115 g (½ cup) sugar
5 g (1 tsp) baking powder
2.5 g (½ tsp) baking soda
2.5 g (½ tsp) salt
120 g (½ cup) sour cream
110 ml (½ cup) vegetable oil
60 ml (4 tbsp) 3.25% milk
15 ml (1 tbsp) vanilla extract
1 large egg
60 g (½ cup) macadamia nuts, chopped
60 g (½ cup) miniature semi-sweet chocolate chips

Preheat oven to 190°C (375°F).

Line muffin pan with muffin cups or use a silicone muffin pan.

In a mixer with a paddle attachment, combine flour, sugar, baking powder, baking soda, and salt and blend well. Add sour cream, vegetable oil, milk, vanilla, and egg. Stir just until dry ingredients are moistened. Fold in macadamia nuts and chocolate chips.

Fill muffin cups ¾ of the way to the top. Sprinkle with streusel mixture. Bake at 190°C (375°F) for eighteen to twenty minutes or until a toothpick inserted in the center comes out clean.

Let muffins cool for five minutes and then remove from pans and cool on rack.

Muffins can be kept at room temperature for two days.

Chocolate Cupcakes

Yield: 12 cupcakes
Preparation time: forty-five minutes

Ingredients:
60 ml (4 tbsp) vegetable oil
170 g (1¼ cups) sugar
1 large egg
5 ml (1 tsp) vanilla extract
1 pinch salt
1 pinch cinnamon (optional)
5 g (1 tsp) baking soda
158 ml (¾ cup) 3.25% milk
30 ml (2 tbsp) lemon juice
40 g (2½ tbsp) cocoa powder
110 g (1⅓ cups) all-purpose flour

Preheat oven to 177°C (350°F).

Combine milk and lemon juice in a cup and allow the mixture to curdle.

In a mixer with a paddle attachment, combine oil, sugar, and egg until smooth. Add vanilla, salt, and baking soda. Mix until well blended. Add curdled milk. Mix in cocoa powder and flour. Scrape the sides and bottom of the mixing bowl. Mix for three minutes.

Divide batter equally between twelve paper-lined cupcakes.

Bake at 177°C (350°F) for twenty-five minutes or until a toothpick inserted in the center comes out clean. Let cool in pan on a rack for twenty minutes. Remove and place on platter to continue cooling. Frost the cupcake with desired topping.

Cupcakes can be kept at room temperature for two days.

Tip: You may add nuts or dried fruits. You may also use butter cream frosting.

Chocolate Fudge Cupcakes

Yield: 24 cupcakes
Preparation time: forty-five minutes

Chocolate Fudge Cupcakes

Ingredients:

250 g (2½ cups) all-purpose flour
5 g (1 tsp) baking soda
5 g (1 tsp) baking powder
5 g (1 tsp) salt
115 g (½ cup) unsalted butter
340 g (1¾ cups) sugar

5 g (1 tsp) vanilla extract
2 large eggs
257 ml (1 cup) 3.25% milk
15 ml (1 tbsp) vinegar
86 g (6 tbsp) hot tap water
60 g (4 tbsp) cocoa powder

Preheat oven to 177°C (350°F).

Place cupcake liners into cupcake tins.

Sift together flour, baking soda, baking powder, and salt onto waxed paper.

In a mixer, cream together butter, sugar, and vanilla until light and fluffy. Add eggs. Beat until well mixed. Mix in flour mixture, vinegar, and milk.

Stir together hot water and cocoa powder in a small bowl until smooth. Add to batter. Beat two minutes at medium speed, scraping the sides of bowl as needed.

Divide batter into prepared cups. Use approximately ¼ cup for each. Bake in preheated oven for twenty-two to twenty-five minutes or until a toothpick inserted in the center comes out clean. Remove cupcakes from pan and let cool to room temperature on wire rack.

Use a pastry knife to frost the cupcakes.

Chocolate Ganache Frosting

Ingredients:
600 g (4 cups) 58% dark chocolate in pistole form or chopped into small pieces
500 ml (2 cups) 35% cream
180 g (¾ cup) unsalted butter

In a saucepan, combine cream and butter and bring to a boil. Pour into the chocolate and stir until a smooth texture is obtained. Keep at room temperature until completely cooled.

Cupcakes can be kept at room temperature for two days.

Tip: Use decorations, such as chocolate vermicelli, chocolate shavings, dried fruits, or fresh raspberries.

Brownie Brownie

Yield: 24 servings
Preparation time: forty-five minutes

Brownies

Ingredients:
150 g (1½ cups) all-purpose flour
330 g (1½ cups) sugar
60 g (4 tbsp) cocoa powder
5 g (1 tsp) baking powder
5 ml (1 tsp) vanilla extract
170 g (¾ cup) unsalted butter
90 ml (6 tbsp) boiling water
3 large eggs
120 g (¾ cup) 50% dark chocolate in pistole form or chopped into small pieces
150 g (1½ cups) chopped walnuts or pecans

Preheat oven to 177°C (350°F).

Line a 13 inch × 9 inch (33 cm × 23 cm) cake pan with greaseproof paper or another nonstick paper.

Melt butter in a saucepan.

In a mixer with a paddle attachment, combine flour, sugar, cocoa powder, baking powder, and vanilla extract. Add eggs one by one. At low speed, mix in melted butter and hot water until smooth. Gently mix in chocolate chips and nuts.

Bake in oven at 177°C (350°F) until a wooden toothpick inserted in the center comes out clean, approximately twenty to thirty minutes.

Let cool. Ice brownie with chocolate frosting.

Frosting

Ingredients:
75 g (⅓ cup) unsalted butter
220 g (1½ cups) sweet or semi-sweet 58% dark chocolate in pistole form or chopped into small pieces
30 g (2 tbsp) light corn syrup
30 ml (2 tbsp) hot espresso or very strong coffee

In a stainless steel bowl, mix butter, chocolate, corn syrup, and coffee. Place the mixture on a double boiler until the mixture has completely melted. Stir mixture until smooth and let cool at room temperature. Spread over the cake or pipe with a star tip and decorate with candy pearls.

Brownies can be kept at room temperature for two days.

Chocolate Ylang-Ylang Mousse

Yield: 12 servings
Preparation time: forty-five minutes

Ingredients:
lady fingers or sponge cake
fresh raspberries as needed to macerate with Grand Marnier for a minimum of one hour
fresh mint
roasted and crushed almonds
chocolate shavings
8 egg yolks
150 g (¾ cup) sugar
150 ml (¾ cup) water
240 g (1⅓ cups) 70% dark chocolate in pistole form or chopped into small pieces
4–5 drops ylang-ylang oil
500 ml (2 cups) 35% cream

In a large plastic bowl, melt the chocolate slowly in a microwave until it reaches 50°C (122°F). Keep it warm.

In a mixer with a whip attachment, whip the 35% cream until soft peaks form.

In a saucepan, combine sugar and water and bring to a boil. Pour into egg yolks in a mixer with a whip attachment. Whip egg yolks and boiling syrup until foamy or at ribbon stage. Gently fold the yolk mixture into the melted chocolate and add in ylang-ylang oil. Use a spatula to fold in the whipped cream. Do not over mix.

To assemble, place raspberries on the bottoms of 12 red wine glasses. Using a piping bag, pipe in a layer of chocolate mousse. Add a layer of sponge cake or lady finger, then a layer of raspberry, and finish with a layer of chocolate mousse.

Let set in the fridge for half an hour. For serving, sprinkle with crushed almonds and decorate with a mint leaf and chocolate shavings.

This mousse can be kept in the fridge for two days.

Jasmine Tea Chocolate Tart

Yield: two 8 inch tarts
Preparation time: forty-five minutes

Tarts

Ingredients:
2 frozen or ready-baked pie shells, or homemade pie or tart shells (see *Sweet Dough Tart Shells* recipe)
Jasmine tea chocolate ganache filling
Jasmine Tea Chocolate Ganache Filling
Ingredients:
780 ml (3¼ cups) 35% cream
6 bags Jasmine tea
180 g (¾ cup) corn syrup
160 g (¾ cup) unsalted butter, at room temperature
2 vanilla beans (split open lengthwise; use only the seeds)
870 g (5⅔ cups) 64% dark chocolate in pistole form or chopped into small pieces

Simmer cream and tea bags in a saucepan. Infuse for five minutes and drain tea bags. Add corn syrup and vanilla seeds and reheat cream to 90°C (194°F). Pour the hot cream over the chocolate and use an electric hand blender to smooth the ganache. Add butter and mix well. Fill the tart shells with ganache and refrigerate for twenty to thirty minutes.

Serve with chocolate ice cream or frozen raspberry yogurt.

Tarts can be refrigerated for three days.

Tiramisu Chocolate Mousse

Yield: 6 portions
Preparation time: forty-five minutes

Ingredients:
Olive oil chocolate cake (see *Olive Oil Chocolate Cake* recipe)
Tiramisu syrup
Chocolate tiramisu cream

Tiramisu Syrup

Ingredients:
200 g (¾ cup) water
250 g (1¼ cups) sugar
15 g (1 tbsp) instant coffee

In a saucepan, combine water, sugar, and instant coffee and bring to a boil. Make sure sugar is completely dissolved. Let cool and add the following ingredients:

50 ml (2½ tbsp) Tia Maria
50 ml (2½ tbsp) coffee liquor
50 ml (2½ tbsp) Grand Marnier
50 ml (2½ tbsp) rum
50 ml (2½ tbsp) Bailey's

Use this tiramisu syrup to soak the olive oil chocolate cake for the tiramisu recipe.

Chocolate Tiramisu

Ingredients:
100 g (¾ cup) 65% dark chocolate in pistole form or chopped into small pieces
300 ml (1⅓ cups) 35% cream
500 g (2 cups) mascarpone cream
150 g (¾ cup) sugar

Melt chocolate in a plastic bowl over a water bath or in a microwave and keep it at 40°C (104°F).

In a mixer with a whip attachment, combine mascarpone, cream, and sugar and whip until soft peaks form. Using a rubber spatula, fold the chocolate into the mascarpone cream.

To assemble, put one thin layer of chocolate cake on the bottom of the 10 inch Pyrex pan. Soak the cake with tiramisu syrup and spread a thin layer of mascarpone cream over the surface. Repeat this process until the pan has been filled to the top. Sift a thin layer of cocoa powder over the surface and chill half an hour before serving.

Tiramisu can be refrigerated for two days.

Tip: For extra coffee flavor, mix equal parts cocoa powder and espresso coffee for the top layer.

Chocolate Ginger Crème Brûlée

Yield: 12 regular ramekins of crème brûlée
Preparation time: twenty minutes, baking time thirty to forty-five minutes

Ingredients:
1 L (4 cups) 35% cream
125 ml (½ cup) 3.25% milk
5–10 g (1-2 tsp) freshly ground ginger
150 g (¾ cup) sugar
12 egg yolks
150 g (1 cup) 64% dark chocolate in pistole form or chopped into small pieces
1 pinch sea salt

Preheat oven to 149°C (300°F).

In a large bowl, whip egg yolks and sugar.

In a saucepan, combine cream, milk, ginger and salt and bring to a boil. Pour into egg yolk mixture and whisk. Use a sifter to drain the cream/egg mixture over the chocolate (to prevent lumps). Mix well using an electric hand blender to ensure the chocolate is melted and mixed into the crème brûlée mix.

Fill ramekins and bake in a water bath at 149°C (300°F) for thirty to forty-five minutes. Let cool and refrigerate for a minimum of one hour before serving.

For serving, sprinkle a little bit of sugar on the top and use a crème brûlée torch to caramelise the sugar. Decorate with a quenelle of whipped cream and fresh berries.

Crème brûlée can be refrigerated for three days.

Tip: Always place a towel on the tray before placing the ramekins on it, and then add water to make a water bath. This is to prevent the ramekins coming into direct contact with the metal, which will give better cooking results.

White Chocolate Orange Crème Brûlée

Yield: 12 regular ramekins of crème brulée
Preparation time: twenty minutes, baking time thirty to forty-five minutes

Ingredients:
1 L (4 cups) 35% cream
25 g (2 tbsp) orange zest
12 egg yolks
100 g (½ cup) sugar
200 g (1½ cups) white chocolate in pistole form or chopped into small pieces

Preheat oven to 149°C (300°F).

In a large bowl, whip egg yolks and sugar.

In a saucepan, combine cream and orange zest and bring to a boil. Pour into the egg yolk mixture and whisk. Use a sifter to drain the cream/egg mixture over the chocolate (to prevent lumps). Mix well using an electric hand blender to ensure the chocolate is melted and mixed into the crème brûlée mix.

Fill ramekins and bake in a water bath at149°C (300°F) for thirty to forty-five minutes. Let cool and refrigerate for a minimum of one hour before serving.

For serving, sprinkle a little bit of sugar on the top and use a crème brûlée torch to caramelise the sugar. Decorate with a quenelle of whipped cream and fresh berries.

Crème brûlée can be refrigerated for three days.

Tip: Add a teaspoon of raspberry jam or orange jelly to the bottom of the ramekins.

Chocolate Green Tea Crème Brûlée

Yield: 12 regular ramekins of crème brulée
Preparation time: twenty minutes, baking time thirty to forty-five minutes

Ingredients:
1 L (4 cups) 35% cream
6 bags green tea
12 egg yolks
150 g (¾ cup) sugar
100 g (¾ cup) 65% dark chocolate in pistole form or chopped into small pieces

Preheat oven to 149°C (300°F).

In a large bowl, whip egg yolks and sugar.

In a saucepan, combine cream and tea bags and bring to a boil. Allow to infuse for five minutes and then drain tea bags. Pour into egg yolk mixture and whisk. Use a sifter to drain the cream/egg mixture over the chocolate (to prevent lumps). Mix well using an electric hand blender to ensure the chocolate is melted and mixed into the crème brûlée mix.

Fill ramekins and bake in a water bath at149°C (300°F) for thirty to forty-five minutes. Let cool and refrigerate for a minimum of one hour before serving.

For serving, sprinkle a little bit of sugar on the top and use a crème brûlée torch to caramelise the sugar. Decorate with a quenelle of whipped cream and fresh berries.

Crème brûlée can be refrigerated for three days.

Tip: For a more intense green tea flavor, put the tea bags into cold cream and refrigerate overnight for maceration. Boil the cream and allow to infuse for five minutes before draining the tea bags. Pour cream into egg yolk mixture and whisk. Use a sifter to drain the cream/egg mixture over the chocolate (to prevent lumps). Mix well using an electric hand blender to ensure the chocolate is melted and mixed into the crème brûlée mix.

Chocolate Lava Cake with Lavender Center

Yield: 10 portions
Preparation time: forty-five minutes, baking time ten minutes

Lavender Centers

Ingredients:
85 ml (¼ cup) 35% cream
4–5 drops lavender oil
115 g (½ cup) 58% dark
chocolate in pistole form or
chopped into small pieces
10 g (2 tsp) unsalted butter

In a saucepan, bring cream to a boil. Pour cream over chocolate mixture, and use an electric hand blender to ensure the ganache is combined smoothly. Add butter and lavender oil and mix well. Pour into ice cube molds pre-lined with plastic wrap. Place in a freezer for a couple of hours until the centers can be easily removed from the mold.

The lavender centers can be prepared a couple days ahead of time. Freeze until needed.

Lava Cake

Ingredients:
400 g (2¾ cups) 58% dark chocolate in pistole
form or chopped into small pieces
23 g (1 cup) unsalted butter
2 tsp vanilla extract
6 egg yolks
6 egg whites
85 g (1 cup) sifted cake flour
2 pinches salt
2 pinches cream of tartar
115 g (½ cup) sugar

Preheat oven to 190°C (375°F).

Apply a thin coat of butter inside 10 ramekins and dust with cocoa powder. You may alternatively use 4 oz aluminum cups.

In a bowl, combine chocolate couverture and butter. Melt over a simmering water bath. Remove from heat. Add vanilla extract and egg yolks. Whisk together until smooth. Using a spatula, gently incorporate the cake flour into the chocolate mixture.

In a mixer, whip egg whites, salt, and cream of tartar until soft peaks form, and then gradually sprinkle in sugar.

Using a rubber spatula, gently fold the egg whites into the chocolate mixture, ⅓ at a time. Fill the ramekins with the batter ¾ of the way to the top. Insert a chocolate lava center into the center of each portion of batter. Place the ramekins in a freezer for twenty minutes.

Bake frozen ramekins at 190°C (375°F) for fifteen minutes. Do not over bake. Remove from oven and let cool for five minutes, and then remove from ramekins and place on serving plate.

Tip: Serve warm with vanilla ice cream on top. To reheat, simply microwave for thirty seconds.

Chocolate Banana Cake

Yield: two 3 inch × 5 inch loaf pans
Preparation time: thirty minutes

Ingredients:
150 g (1½ cups) pastry flour
50 g (½ cup) all-purpose flour
160 g (¾ cup) sugar
80 ml (5 tbsp vegetable oil
1 pinch salt
1 pinch baking soda
2 pinches baking powder
40 g (¼ cup) walnuts
90 ml (6 tbsp) 3.25% milk
40 g (1½ tbsp) corn syrup
2 large eggs
200 g (1 cup) very ripe banana
75 g (¾ cup) chocolate chips

Preheat oven to 163°C (325°F).

In a mixer with a paddle attachment, mix all ingredients accordingly. Do not over mix. Pour into cake pans or loaf pans greased with oil spray or melted butter and lightly floured. Bake for twenty to twenty-five minutes.

Optional: Decorate with a glaze of cold dark chocolate fondue on top.

Tie-wrapped banana cake can be kept at room temperature for two days.

Tip: The cake is done when a wooden toothpick inserted into the center of the cake comes out clean.

Fruit Cake

Yield: four 3 inch × 5 inch loaf pans
Preparation time: one hour, plus an overnight soak for the raisins.

Ingredients:
325 g (1⅓ cups) butter
325 g (1½ cups) icing sugar
15 large eggs
1 tsp lemon zest
1 tsp orange zest
100 g (¼ cup) dried golden raisins
100 g (¼ cup) dried sultana raisins
100 g (¼ cup) candied orange peel
12 g (1 tbsp) chopped candied ginger
450 g (3½ cups) pastry flour
15 g (1 tbsp) baking powder
2 g (2 pinches) sea salt
75 g (¾ cup) 70% dark chocolate in pistole form or chopped into small pieces

Soak raisins in boiling water for one hour. Drain raisins and soak in rum overnight.

Preheat oven to 205°C (400°F).

In a mixer with a paddle attachment, cream together butter, icing sugar, eggs (one by one), and zests until a smooth and creamy mixture is obtained. Fold in by hand, raisins, candied orange peels, ginger, sifted flour, salt, baking powder, and chocolate. Fill cake pans or loaf pans lined with parchment paper until they are ¾ of the way full. Sprinkle the top with sliced almonds.

Place in oven and reduce temperature to 150°C (300°F). Bake twenty-five to thirty minutes.

Tie-wrapped fruit cake can be kept at room temperature for two days.

Tip: Insert a toothpick into the center of the cake. When it comes out clean, the cake is done.

Bourdaloue Pear Tart

Yield: two 8 inch tarts
Preparation time: forty-five minutes

Ingredients:
6 fresh pears (Forelle, Anjou, or Bartlett), peeled and cut into halves
    and sliced horizontally, or pear in light syrup
Two 8 inch tart shells (see *Sweet Dough Tart Shells* recipe)
Almond cream

Frangipane Cream (Almond Cream)

Ingredients:
250 g (2 cups) almond powder
250 g (1 cup) unsalted butter at room temperature
250 g (2 cups) icing sugar
2 large eggs
100 g (½ cup) 64% dark chocolate in pistole form or chopped into small pieces
45 ml (3 tbsp) dark rum

Preheat oven to 205°C (400°F).

In a mixer with a paddle attachment, sift together almond powder and icing sugar, and then add butter. Cream the mixture together, and then add eggs one by one. Continue to mix until a smooth and creamy texture is obtained. Add rum and chocolate.

To assemble, put two 8 inch tart shells on a sheet pan. Use a piping bag or spatula with a circular motion, covering the bottoms of the tart shells with frangipane cream. Arrange the pears on top of the frangipane (you can cover the entire surface if you wish). Top with almond slices.

Place in oven and reduce temperature to 163°C (325°F). Bake until the almond cream is golden brown.

The tart can be refrigerated for four days.

Tip: Serve warm with a scoop of vanilla ice cream, or serve cold with warm chocolate fondue (see *Chocolate Fondue* recipe).

White Chocolate Lemon Meringue Tart

Yield: two 8 inch tarts
Preparation time: forty-five minutes

Ingredients:
Two 8 inch tart shells (see *Sweet Dough Tart Shells* recipe)
White chocolate lemon cream
Lemon tart meringue

White Chocolate Lemon Cream

Ingredients:
1 tsp lemon zest
250 g (1 cup) lemon juice
7 egg yolks

3 large eggs
100 g (½ cup) sugar
170 g (¾ cup) unsalted butter at room temperature
100 g (¾ cup) white chocolate in pistole form or chopped into small pieces

In a saucepan, combine lemon zest, lemon juice, egg yolks, eggs, and sugar and bring to a boil. Continue to stir to prevent the cream from burning. Add chocolate and mix well. Let the cream cool down to 40°C (104°F). Add butter. Mix well using an electric hand blender.

Fill the tart shells evenly. Refrigerate for one hour before putting the meringue on top.

Lemon Tart Meringue

Ingredients:
5 egg whites
300 g (1½ cups) sugar

Preheat oven to 216°C (420°F).

In a stainless steel bowl over a double boiler, combine egg whites and sugar. Whip until sugar is completely dissolved in the egg whites. Transfer the hot liquid mixture to a mixing bowl. Using a mixer with a whip attachment, whip the meringue to a firm stage. Using a spatula or piping bag, cover the tarts with meringue. Put the tarts into the oven for three minutes or until the meringue becomes golden.

You can also use a crème brûlée torch to brown the meringue.

The tart can be refrigerated for four days.

Tip: Make the meringue just before serving. Serve with lemon or orange sherbet in the summertime.

Chocolate Macaroon with Milk Chocolate Raspberry

Yield: 50 macaroons
Preparation time: forty-five minutes

Macaroons

Ingredients:
7 egg whites
50 g (⅓ cup) icing sugar
5 ml (1 tsp) lemon juice
450 g (3½ cups) icing sugar
250 g (2 cups) almond powder
40 g (2½ tbsp) cocoa powder

Preheat the oven to 150°C (300°F).

In a large bowl, use a hand whip to mix together 450 g (3½ cups) of icing sugar, almond powder, and cocoa powder.

In a mixer with a whip attachment, whip egg whites, 50 g (⅓ cup) of icing sugar, and lemon juice to a firm meringue.

Using a spatula, gently fold the dry ingredients into the meringue to obtain a smooth and shiny texture. Using a piping bag with a round tip, pipe the macaroon mixture onto parchment paper or a silicone mat into ¾ inch diameter or desired size. Let dry at room temperature for twenty minutes.

Bake fifteen minutes. Allow macaroons to cool, and then sandwich them with raspberry filling.

Tip: Food colorings maybe added to create colorful macaroon shells.

Milk Chocolate Raspberry Filling

Ingredients:
150 g (1 cup) raspberry purée
300 g (2 cups) milk chocolate in pistole form or chopped into small pieces
40 g (2½ tbsp) corn syrup
50 g (4 tbsp) unsalted butter at room temperature
15 g (1 tbsp) raspberry liquor

In a large bowl, add milk chocolate couverture.

In a saucepan, combine raspberry purée and corn syrup and bring to a boil. Pour the boiling liquid over the chocolate. Use an electric hand blender to mix until smooth. Add butter and raspberry liquor. Continue to use the hand blender to emulsify the ganache. Allow ganache to cool. Use a piping bag to pipe the filling into the center of two macaroons.

Macaroons can be kept in the freezer for one month or refrigerated for two days.

Banana Caramel Chocolate Crêpe

Yield: 40 crêpes
Preparation time: forty-five minutes

Ingredients:
Crêpe chocolat à l'ancienne (see *Crêpe Chocolat à l'ancienne* recipe)
Vanilla pastry cream (see *Vanilla Pastry Cream* recipe)
Caramel banana flambé

Caramel Banana Flambé

Ingredients:
8 bananas (not too ripe)
60 ml (4 tbsp) lime juice
250 g (1¼ cups) sugar
30 g (2 tbsp) butter
60 ml (4 tbsp) dark rum

Peel the bananas and cut into slices. Squeeze lime juice over the bananas to prevent browning.

In a frying pan on high heat, add half of the sugar. Stir until it starts to melt and caramelise. Slowly add the remaining sugar and continue to stir. Once it's caramelised, add butter and bananas. Quickly sauté to prevent the bananas from softening. Add rum and flambé the caramel bananas.

To assemble, place a crêpe in the middle of a dessert plate. Use a piping bag or a tablespoon to put the pastry cream in the center. Top with a couple slices of banana. Fold the crêpe to form a pillow shape. Decorate with a scoop of vanilla ice cream and some caramel sauce. Top with a fresh mint leaf.

Lime Macaroon

Yield: 50 macaroons
Preparation time: forty-five minutes

Macaroons

Ingredients:
7 egg whites	450 g (3½ cups) icing sugar
50 g (⅓ cup) icing sugar	290 g (2¼ cups) almond powder
5 ml (1 tsp) lemon juice	Green food color as needed

Preheat the oven at 150°C (300°F).

In a large bowl, use a hand whip to mix together 450 g (3½ cups) icing sugar and almond powder.

In a mixer with a whip attachment, whip egg whites, 50 g (⅓ cup) sugar, and lemon juice to a firm meringue.

Using a spatula, gently fold the dry ingredients into the meringue to obtain a smooth and shiny texture. Add green color to the dough. Using a piping bag with a round tip, pipe the macaroon mixture onto parchment paper or a silicone mat into ¾ inch diameter or desired size. Let dry at room temperature for twenty minutes.

Bake for fifteen minutes. Allow macaroons to cool, and then sandwich them with lime ganache.

Lime Ganache

Ingredients:
5 g (1 tsp) lime zest	50 g (3½ tbsp) sugar
80 ml (6 tbsp) lime juice	375 g (2¾ cups) white chocolate in pistole form or chopped into small pieces
4 egg yolks	90 g (6 tbsp) butter
	15 ml (1 tbsp) vodka

Place white chocolate couverture, butter, and vodka in a large bowl.

In a saucepan, combine lime juice, zest, egg yolks, and sugar and bring to a boil. Pour into chocolate mixture and use an electric hand blender to emulsify the ganache. Allow ganache to cool. Use a piping bag to pipe the filling into the center of two macaroons.

Macaroons can be kept in the freezer for one month or refrigerated for two days.

Almond Sponge Cake

Yield: 6 muffin sized cakes
Preparation time: thirty minutes

Ingredients:
200 g (1 cup) almond paste (mazipan)
4 large eggs
30 g (2 tbsp) melted butter
15 g (1 tbsp) pastry flour
15 g (1 tbsp) cocoa powder
2.5 g (½ tsp) baking powder
5 g (2 tsp) lemon zest
50 g (½ cup) 58% dark chocolate in pistole form or chopped into small pieces

Preheat oven to 177°C (350°F).

Grease muffin pans.

Using a mixer with a paddle attachment, on medium speed, cream almond paste together with eggs, one by one. Add flour, cocoa powder, and baking powder. Continue to mix at low speed. Add melted butter, lemon zest, and chocolate.

Pour the mixture into the muffin pans, filling to the top. Bake at 177°C (350°F) for fifteen minutes or until a toothpick inserted in the center comes out clean. Remove cakes from muffin pans and allow them to cool on a wire rack.

Serve with ice cream or chocolate fondue (see *Chocolate Fondue* recipe).

Cake can be kept at room temperature for two days.

Financier with Chocolate Pastry Cream

Yield: 6 muffin sized cakes
Preparation time: thirty minutes

Hazelnut butter

Ingredients:
150 g butter

Place 150 g (¾ cup) of butter in a saucepan and bring to a boil. Keep boiling until butter turns golden brown and starts to smell like roasted hazelnuts. Remove from heat and strain through a coffee filter. Use while warm.

Financier

Ingredients:
63 g (½ cup) almond powder
225 g (1½ cups) icing sugar
82 g (½ cup) pastry flour
2.5 g (½ tsp) baking powder
5 g (1 tsp) orange zest
6 egg whites
20 g (1 tbsp) honey
100 ml (½ cup) hazelnut butter

Preheat oven to 177°C (350°F).

In a large bowl, sift together flour, icing sugar, and baking powder. Using a hand whip, mix in almond powder, orange zest, honey, egg whites, and hazelnut butter.

Spoon into greased muffin pans or silicone molds. Bake for fifteen to twenty minutes or until a toothpick inserted in the center comes out clean.

Allow to cool on a rack. Serve with chocolate pastry cream (see *Vanilla Chocolate Pastry Cream* recipe).

Belgian Chocolate Waffle

Yield: 12 waffles
Preparation time: thirty minutes

Ingredients:
280 g (2½ cups) all-purpose flour
55 g (3½ tbsp) cocoa powder
3 g (½ tsp) salt
8 g (1½ tsp) baking powder
10 g (2 tbsp) sugar
2 large eggs
340 ml (1½ cups) 3.25% milk
165 ml (¾ cup) water
65 ml (4 tbsp) melted unsalted butter

In a large bowl, sift together all the dry ingredients.

Using a hand whip, mix all the liquids with the dry ingredients. Refrigerate for one hour. Bake in a waffle iron for five minutes.

Tip: Serve with whipped cream, chocolate fondue, and fresh fruits.

Chocolate Peanut Butter Spread

Yield: 8 cups
Preparation time: thirty minutes

Ingredients:
200 g (1 cup) sugar
75 g (¼ cup) corn syrup
780 ml (3¼ cups) 35% cream
350 g (2 cups) milk chocolate in pistole form or chopped into small pieces
100 g (½ cup) 75% dark chocolate in pistole form or chopped into small pieces
200 g (1 cup) natural peanut butter

In a saucepan, heat the cream and keep it warm.

In a large bowl, combine the milk chocolate and dark chocolate couvertures and peanut butter.

In a separate saucepan, cook sugar and corn syrup until it caramelises. Slowly add the hot cream to deglaze the caramel. Pour hot caramel into the chocolate and peanut butter mixture. Use an electric hand blender to combine all ingredients. Pour into jars and allow cooling down completely before capping. This is to prevent the mold forming from the moisture.

Keep in the fridge for six hours before serving.

Chocolate peanut butter spread can be refrigerated for two weeks.

Crèmeux Chocolat aux Framboises

Yield: enough to fill 12 champagne flutes
Preparation time: one hour

Raspberries in Grand Marnier

Ingredients:
3 pints fresh raspberries
100 ml (7 tbsp) Grand Marnier liquor
70 g (5½ tbsp) sugar
70 ml (5½ tbsp) water

In a salad bowl, wash and drain the raspberries.

In a saucepan, combine water and sugar and bring to a boil. Allow to cool to room temperature. Add liquor. Pour over the raspberries, and let the mixture macerate overnight in the fridge.

Raspberry Coulis

Ingredients:
430 g (2 cups) raspberry purée
20 ml (4 tsp) lemon juice
90 g (6 tbsp) sugar
22 g (1½ tbsp) corn starch
22 g (1½ tbsp) sugar
50 g (3½ tbsp) cocoa butter
30 ml (2 tbsp) Grand Marnier liquor

Sift together the corn starch and 22 g (1½ tbsp) sugars.

In a saucepan, combine raspberry purée, 90 g (6 tbsp) sugar, and lemon juice and bring to a boil. Using a hand whip, whip in corn starch with 22 g (1½ tbsp) sugar. Continue whipping until the coulis reaches 90°C (194°F). Remove from heat. While continuing to whip, mix in cocoa butter and liquor.

Allow coulis to cool to room temperature. Using a piping bag or milkshake spoon, place 2 tbsp of coulis in the bottom of each flute. Refrigerate while preparing the chocolate mousse.

Chocolate Mousse

Ingredients:
100 g (½ cup) sugar
60 ml (4 tbsp) water
7 egg yolks
220 g (1½ cups) 66% dark chocolate in pistole form or chopped into small pieces
720 ml (3¼ cups) 35% cream

Place chocolate couverture in a plastic bowl and melt it in the microwave. Keep it warm.

In a mixer with a whip attachment, whip cream until soft peaks form. Place in the fridge.

In a mixer with a whip attachment, whip the egg yolks at medium speed.

In a saucepan, combine sugar and water and bring to a boil. Pour into the yolks. Turn the mixer on at maximum speed and whip to ribbon stage. Using a plastic spatula, gently fold in melted hot chocolate, and then fold in the whipped cream in two stages.

To assemble, put a layer of raspberries in Grand Marnier on top of the coulis in the flute glasses. Using a piping bag, fill the flutes with chocolate mousse to ¾ full. Spoon a thin layer of coulis on top and decorate with fresh fruits and mint leaves.

Crèmeux chocolat aux framboises can be refrigerated for two days.

Passion Mandarin

Yield: enough to fill 12 red wines glasses
Preparation time: one hour

Ingredients:
Lady fingers
Crème de mandarine

Passion mousse
Two 10 oz cans of mandarin segments in syrup for decoration
Whipped cream.

Mandarin purée

For mandarin purée, open three cans of mandarins (10 oz) and drain off syrup. Place mandarins in a food processor and reduce to a purée. Reserve in a plastic container.

Crème de Mandarine

Ingredients:
485 ml (2 cups) 35% cream
85 g (7 tbsp) sugar
20 g (4 tsp) corn starch
4 large eggs

250 g (1⅓ cups) mandarin purée
120 g (½ cup) unsalted butter
45 g (½ cup) cocoa butter
30 ml (2 tbsp) Mandarin Napoleon liquor

In a mixer with a whip attachment, whip cream until soft peaks form. Place in the fridge.

In a small bowl, sift together sugar and corn starch. Using a hand whip, whip the eggs into the mixture.

Place the mandarin purée in a saucepan and bring to a boil. Using a hand whip, mix in the sugar, corn starch, and egg mixture. Keep whipping until the mixture begins bubbling. Remove from heat. Add butter and cocoa butter, and whip with a hand whip until the mixture becomes a smooth crème. Allow crème to cool to room temperature. Using a hand whip, gently fold in the Mandarin liquor and whipped cream.

Using a piping bag or spoon, fill 12 red wine glasses ⅓ of the way full with the crème. Refrigerate for thirty minutes to allow the crème to set. In the meantime, prepare the passion mousse.

White Chocolate Mousse

Yield: enough to fill 16 4-oz dessert glasses
Preparation time: forty-five minutes

Ingredients:
500 g (2 cups) pastry cream (see *Vanilla Pastry Cream* recipe)
12 lime Macaroons
Whipped cream
Chocolate pearls
500 g (2 cups) vanilla pastry cream
400 g (2¾ cups) white chocolate in pistole form or chopped into small pieces
750 g (3 cups) 35% cream

In a mixer with a whip attachment, whip the cream until soft peaks form. Place in the fridge.

Place white chocolate in a large bowl and melt in the microwave.

Using a hand whip, mix the pastry cream into the hot white chocolate. Using a plastic spatula, gently fold the whipped cream, in 2 separate amounts, into the pastry cream mixture.

Using a piping bag or tablespoon, fill 16 dessert glasses ¾ of the way full with the mousse. Allow thirty minutes for the mousse to set in the fridge. Decorate with a quenelle of whipped cream, a macaroon, and chocolate pearls.

White chocolate mousse can be refrigerated for three days.

Pot de Crème au Chocolat

Yield: enough to fill 12 ramekins or 3 oz dessert glasses
Preparation time: twenty minutes, cooking time one hour

Ingredients:
1 L (4 cups) 3.25% milk
150 g (¾ cup) sugar
220 g (1½ cups) 70% dark chocolate in pistole form or chopped into small pieces
2 large eggs
4 egg yolks

Preheat oven to 120°C (250°F).

In a stainless steel bowl, whip together egg yolks and whole eggs using a hand whip.

Place milk and sugar in a saucepan and bring to a boil. Add chocolate couverture. Use a hand whip to mix until chocolate is completely melted. Pour into the egg mixture. Use a hand blender to mix until evenly blended.

Place a small towel in the bottom of a 16 inch × 24 inch cake pan. Fill twelve ramekins or dessert glasses ¾ of the way with the cream mixture.

Add hot water to the pan until it is halfway up the sides of the ramekins. Carefully place the pan in the oven and bake for one hour.

Remove pan from oven. Allow the water bath to cool down. Take out the pots de crème au chocolat and refrigerate them for one hour before serving. Serve with a quenelle of whipped cream.

Pots de crème au chocolat can be refrigerated for two days.

Basic Recipes

Olive Oil Chocolate Cake

Yield: 16 inch × 12 inch baking tray
Preparation time: twenty-five minutes

Ingredients:
360 g (3⅔ cups) all-purpose flour
360 g (1¾ cups) sugar
4 pinches salt
60 g (6 tbsp) cocoa powder
12 g (1 tbsp) baking soda
200 g (¾ cup) olive oil
10 g (2 tsp) vanilla extract
600 g (2⅔ cups) 3.25% milk
35 g (2 tbsp) vinegar

Preheat oven to 158°C (315°F).

Butter and flour a 16 inch × 12 inch cake pan, or use an oil spray.

Sift all dry ingredients together. Combine all liquids *except the vinegar.*

Using a hand blender, mix all the dry and liquid (*except the vinegar*) ingredients together, and then add the vinegar to the liquid cake base and mix until smooth. Immediately pour into the cake pan and bake. *Do not wait or adjust the recipe*; this cake batter is very fluid.

Bake for twenty-five to thirty minutes. Cool on a wire rack and then cut into small cubes.

Tip: Insert a toothpick into the center of the cake. When it comes out clean, the cake is done.

Sweet Dough Tart Shells

Yield: three 8 inch tart shells
Preparation time: thirty minutes

Ingredients:
270 g (1¾ cups) icing sugar
270 g (1 cup and 6 tbsp) unsalted butter, at room temperature
2 large eggs
400 g (4 cups) pastry flour
50 g (5½ tbsp) cocoa powder (optional for chocolate dough)

Preheat oven to 191°C (375°F).

Using your hands, combine butter with icing sugar and mix well. Incorporate the eggs. Add flour and/or cocoa powder (pre-sifted) and form dough without over mixing. Refrigerate for one hour.

On a floured surface, roll the dough into a thin layer and place over a pie tin. Let set for thirty minutes in a freezer before baking. Bake until golden.

Tips: Always use pastry flour for sugar dough or pie dough because of its very low gluten content. This helps to prevent shrinkage after baking. Ensure the shell is completely frozen before baking; this helps prevent shrinkage.

Sponge Cake

Yield: 16 inch × 12 inch or two 8 inch cake pans
Preparation time: forty-five minutes

Ingredients:
5 large eggs
15 g (1 tbsp) milk powder
5 g (1 tsp) salt
5 ml (1 tsp) vanilla extract
825 g (4¼ cups) sugar
425 g (4¼ cups) pastry flour
10 g (2 tsp) baking powder

Preheat oven to 190°C (375°F).

In a mixer, combine all ingredients except baking powder. Using a whip attachment, whip the mixture for eight minutes on maximum speed. Add baking powder and whip at medium speed for an additional two minutes.

Line a sheet pan with parchment paper or spray the entire cake pan (shape of your choice) with oil spray, Fill ¾ the pan ¾ of the way. Place the sheet pan in the oven, reset the temperature to 150°C (300°F), and bake until cake is spongy or until a wooden toothpick inserted into the cake comes out clean. Let cake cool on a wire rack and then store in fridge or freezer.

Tip: Sponge cake can be made in advance and stored in the freezer for up to three weeks if it's well wrapped in plastic wrap.

Chocolate Sponge Cake

Yield: 16 inch × 12 inch or two 8 inch cake pans
Preparation time: forty-five minutes

Ingredients:
6 large eggs
150 g (½ cup and 2 tbsp) water
15 g (1 tbsp) milk powder
5 g (1 tsp) salt
5 ml (1 tsp) vanilla extract
425 g (4¼ cups) sugar
400 g (4 cups) pastry flour
60 g (4 tbsp) cocoa powder
10 g (2 tsp) baking powder

Preheat oven to 190°C (375°F).

In a mixer, combine all ingredients except baking powder. Using a whip attachment, whip the mixture for eight minutes on maximum speed. Add baking powder and whip at medium speed for an additional two minutes.

Line a sheet pan with parchment paper or spray the entire cake pan (shape of your choice) with oil spray. Fill ¾ the pan ¾ of the way. Place the sheet pan in the oven, reset the temperature to 150°C (300°F), and bake until cake is spongy or until a wooden toothpick inserted into the cake comes out clean. Let cake cool on a wire rack and then store in fridge or freezer.

Tip: Sponge cake can be made in advance and stored in the freezer for up to three weeks if it's well wrapped in plastic wrap.

Crêpe Parisien

Yield: 40 crêpes
Preparation time: one hour

Ingredients:
275 g (1 cup and 2 tbsp) 3.25% milk
80 g (6 tbsp) vegetable oil
45 g (3 tbsp) Guinness beer
45 g (3 tbsp) sugar
4 large eggs
5 g (1 tsp) salt
256 g (2½ cups) bread flour

Using a hand whip, mix all the liquid ingredients together with sugar, egg, and salt in a large bowl, and then slowly pour in the flour and continue to mix well. Refrigerate for thirty minutes.

In a nonstick frying pan on medium heat, pour in 3 ounces of the crêpes batter, make sure it spreads out evenly on the pan, cook for thirty seconds or until edge is golden brown then flip and continue to cook on the other side for another thirty seconds. Use oil spray as needed.

Tip: Crêpes can be used for savory or dessert dishes.

Crêpe Chocolat à l'ancienne

Yield: 40 crêpes
Preparation time: one hour

Ingredients:
275 g (1 cup and 2 tbsp) 3.25% milk
80 ml (6 tbsp) vegetable oil
45 g (3 tbsp) Guinness beer
45 g (3 tbsp) sugar
4 large eggs
5 g (1 tsp) salt
192 g (1½ cups) bread flour
64 g (2 tbsp) cocoa powder

Using a hand whip, mix all the liquid ingredients together with sugar, egg, and salt in a large bowl, and then slowly pour in the flour and cocoa powder and continue to mix well. Refrigerate for thirty minutes.

In a nonstick frying pan on medium heat, pour in 3 ounces of the crêpes batter, make sure it spreads out evenly on the pan, cook for thirty seconds or until edge is golden brown then flip and continue to cook on the other side for another thirty seconds. Use oil spray as needed.

Serve with ice cream, maple syrup, caramelised banana, fresh fruits, and whipped cream.

Tip: These crêpes can be refrigerated or stored in a freezer.

Vanilla Pastry Cream

Preparation time: forty-five minutes

Ingredients:
1 L (4 cups and 3 tbsp) 3.25% milk
256 g (2 cups) sugar
2 large eggs
6 egg yolks
2 vanilla beans (split open lengthwise; use only the seeds)
100 g (7 tbsp) corn starch
10 g (½ cup) unsalted butter at room temperature

In a mixer with a whip attachment, cream together whole eggs, egg yolks, vanilla seeds, corn starch, and 1 cup of the sugar.

In a saucepan, combine milk with the remaining 1 cup of sugar and bring to a boil. Whip the milk mixture into the egg mixture. Continue whipping until the cream starts to bubble and thicken. Transfer to a large bowl.

Cover with plastic wrap and allow the cream to cool to 40°C (104°F). Add butter and use a hand whip to mix. Place in the fridge.

Tip: Coffee flavors, liquors, and fruits can be added to the pastry cream. Serve cold in a dessert glass or wine glass with lady fingers or sponge cake and chocolate fondue.

Vanilla Chocolate Pastry Cream

Preparation time: forty-five minutes

Ingredients:
1 L (4 cups and 3 tbsp) 3.25% milk
256 g (2 cups) sugar
2 large eggs
6 egg yolks
2 vanilla beans (split open lengthwise; use only the seeds)
100 g (7 tbsp) corn starch
150 g (¾ cup) 58% dark chocolate in pistole form or chopped into small pieces
100 g (½ cup) unsalted butter

In a mixer with a whip attachment, cream together whole eggs, egg yolks, vanilla seeds, corn starch, and half of the sugar.

In a saucepan, combine milk and the remaining sugar and bring to a boil. Whip the milk mixture into the egg mixture. Continue whipping until the cream starts to bubble and thicken. Add the chocolate couverture and use an electric hand blender to mix well. Transfer to a large bowl.

Cover with plastic wrap and allow the cream cool down to 40°C (104°F). Add in butter and use a hand whip to mix. Place in the fridge.

Tips: Coffee flavors, liquors, and fruits can be added to the chocolate pastry cream. Serve cold in dessert glasses or wine glasses with lady fingers or sponge cake and chocolate fondue. You may use a higher percentage of dark chocolate, milk chocolate, or white chocolate.

Buttercream

Yield: 8 cups of buttercream
Preparation time: thirty minutes

Ingredients:
500 g (2 cups) fresh egg whites
600 g (3 cups) sugar
600 g (2½ cups) unsalted butter
150 g (¾ cup) margarine

In a mixer with a whip attachment, cream together butter and margarine until light and smooth. Place in a bowl and reserve.

In a stainless steel bowl, use a hand whip to mix the egg whites and sugar. Put the mixture on a double boiler over medium heat. Keep stirring until the sugar is completely dissolved in the egg whites. Transfer the egg white mixture to a mixer. Using a whip attachment, whip the meringue until it cools down. With the mixer on low speed, gradually add the butter mixture. Turn the mixer to maximum speed and continue to whip for five minutes until a light and smooth buttercream forms.

Tip: For flavor, add melted 70% dark chocolate, peanut butter, jam, or artificial flavors (vanilla, orange, etc.).

CPSIA information can be obtained
at www.ICGtesting.com
230022LV00004B